J 920 PAR
Parker-Rock, Michelle.
Patricia and Fredrick
McKissack

ATE DUE

D1124212

AVON PUBLIC LIBRARY
BOX 977/200 BENCHMARK RD.
AVON, CO 81620

Patricia and Fredrick McKissack

Authors Kids Love

by Michelle Parker-Rock

Enslow Elementary

an imprint of

Enslow Publishers, Inc.

40 Industrial Road
Box 398
Berkeley Heights, NJ 07922
USA

http://www.enslow.com

This book is based on a live interview with Patricia and Fredrick McKissack on September 12–14, 2006.

*For M.O., a tower of strength, and
to P.C.M. and F.L.M, with admiration, respect, and love. Thanks.*

Copyright © 2009 by Michelle Parker-Rock

All rights reserved.

No part of this book may be reproduced by any means without the written permission of the publisher.

Library of Congress Cataloging-in-Publication Data

Parker-Rock, Michelle.
    Patricia and Fredrick McKissack : authors kids love / Michelle Parker-Rock.
    p. cm. — (Authors kids love.)
    "Based on a live interview with Patricia and Fredrick McKissack on September 12–14, 2006"—T.p. verso.
    Summary: "A short biography of this husband and wife writing team, including their relationship, how they became authors, how they write together, and their advice for young, aspiring authors"—Provided by publisher.
    Includes index.
    ISBN-13: 978-0-7660-2759-6
    ISBN-10: 0-7660-2759-7
    1. McKissack, Pat, 1944– —Juvenile literature. 2. McKissack, Pat, 1944– —Interviews. 3. McKissack, Fredrick—Juvenile literature. 4. McKissack, Fredrick—Interviews. 5. Authors, American—20th century—Biography—Juvenile literature. 6. African American authors—Biography—Juvenile literature. 7. African American authors—Interviews. 8. Children's literature—Authorship—Juvenile literature. I. Title.
    PS3563.C38323Z84 2008
    813'.54—dc22
    [B]
                    2008001746

Printed in the United States of America

10 9 8 7 6 5 4 3 2 1

To Our Readers: We have done our best to make sure that all Internet Addresses in this book were active and appropriate when we went to press. However, the author and publisher have no control over and assume no liability for the material available on those Internet sites or on other Web sites they may link to. Any comments or suggestions can be sent by e-mail to comments@enslow.com or to the address on the back cover.

♻ Enslow Publishers, Inc., is committed to printing our books on recycled paper. The paper in every book contains 10% to 30% post-consumer waste (PCW). The cover board on the outside of each book contains 100% PCW. Our goal is to do our part to help young people and the environment too!

Photo Credits: Jaffe Studio, www.haljaffe.com, p. 1; courtesy of Patricia C. and Fredrick L. McKissack, pp. 3, 4, 11, 13, 15, 18, 19, 21, 23, 25, 26, 27, 28, 30, 37, 41, 43, 46; Michelle Parker-Rock © 2006, pp. 8, 36.

Cover Photo: Front cover image by Jaffe Studio, www.haljaffe.com; back cover image courtesy of Patricia C. and Fredrick L. McKissack.

AVON PUBLIC LIBRARY
BOX 977/200 BENCHMARK RD.
AVON, CO 81620

Contents

Authors Patricia and Fredrick McKissack.

Just One Book

In 1976, Patricia McKissack went to Atlanta, Georgia, to attend a meeting of the American Library Association. She was working as an editor for Concordia Publishing, a company in St. Louis, Missouri, that produced religious books for children.

At the conference, people were talking about creating more books for black children, books that would inform all readers about the contributions that African Americans had made to the nation.

"In those days," said Fredrick McKissack, "there were so few books for and about the African-American child. Black kids needed to see themselves in books."

The Coretta Scott King Award

In 1969, a year after civil rights leader Dr. Martin Luther King, Jr., was assassinated, two school librarians, Glyndon Greer and Mabel McKissack, who was not related to Patricia and Fredrick McKissack, met at a conference of the American Library Association. The association is an organization that helps libraries and encourages library education all around the world. The two librarians saw a need for a new book award to recognize African-American authors and illustrators. They created a prize and named it the Coretta Scott King Award, in honor of Dr. King's work for peace and goodwill, and for his wife Coretta, who continued her husband's work. The first award was given in 1970 to Lillie Patterson for her biography *Martin Luther King, Jr.: Man of Peace*.

Patricia said:

As a teacher, I had taught my students about books that won the Newbery, Caldecott, and many other awards, but none of those honors had ever been presented to an author or illustrator of color. The Coretta Scott King Award was important because it specifically recognized African Americans.

Patricia was convinced that something needed to be done. However, she was not yet thinking about writing and publishing any books of her own. She was contemplating her role as an editor. "I thought, 'wouldn't it be great to work on a book that would win the Coretta Scott King Award?'"

Patricia realized that it would be difficult to produce an African-American book at Concordia, because the company was the publishing arm of the Lutheran Church. "My focus was on Arch Books, which were retellings of Bible stories in new and creative ways," she said. "But I did try whenever possible to make sure that there were black children represented in the illustrations. I was successful on a very limited level, but I still made some progress."

Fredrick McKissack, a civil engineer, had a successful construction company called Nimrod, Inc., but by 1981, the building industry was not doing very well. Things had also changed at Concordia. Both Patricia and Fredrick were ready for a change. She said:

Whenever Fred and I needed to talk about something important, we went to the waterfall in Forest Park. It was so calming there. We sat by the rocks and listened to the water crashing and we'd talk. One day, I was very upset, so we went to our spot. Fred asked me, "What would you like to do if you could do anything you wanted to for the rest of your life?" I said, "I would love to write a book for children." He said, "Let's go do that."

The McKissacks by the waterfall in Forest Park where, in 1981, they decided to write just one children's book.

The McKissacks wanted to tell stories that connected them to themselves and to others through shared literary experiences. They believed that the most important stories are the ones we learn in childhood.

"If a child has no stories, he or she doesn't have much of a cultural anchor," said Patricia. "It is from stories that we learn our history, our customs, and our traditions. But if you are denied your stories, as black people were, that causes confusion and a sense of being disconnected."

At the time, the McKissacks' goal was to write just one book. "We never intended to make this a lifetime career," said Patricia, "but as it turns out, twenty-five years later, we have written over a hundred books, and we are still writing."

Chapter 2

Friendship for Today

*P*atricia McKissack was born Patricia L'Ann Carwell in Smyrna, Tennessee, on August 9, 1944, to Robert and Erma Carwell. When Patricia was three, her family moved to St. Louis, where her father worked for an insurance company. He later became a security officer at the airport. Her mother was a housewife, and occasionally she worked as a domestic with Patricia's grandmother, serving food at other people's parties. The Carwells did not have a lot of money, but they were not poor.

People in our community worked as janitors and chauffeurs, or they worked for the railroads. They didn't make a lot of money, but they made a decent living. My parents were pretty much like that, too. There were white families that lived nearby, but we couldn't go to school together because of segregation."

As a child growing up in the South in the 1950s, before the civil rights movement, Patricia was very aware of the fact that she was black. During that time period, black people were referred to as colored or Negro.

Patricia at age six with her mother, Erma Carwell.

Patricia said:

There were signs on stores and restaurants and other businesses and buildings that said that colored people could not go in. I would ask, "Why can't I go in there? Why can't we go to that show?" My mother would tell me it was because we were colored. This is the way it was. As I got older, I came to understand, but I did not think it was fair. My parents said they knew it wasn't fair, but it was the way it was, and we couldn't change it. My mother used to say to us before we went downtown, "All of you go to the bathroom. Sit there until you use it!" I knew what it meant. She was worried that she would have to take us into the alley if we had to go to the bathroom, because there was no place downtown where colored people could go.

Although African Americans could go to the movie theaters for white people, they had to go up the back stairway and sit in the balcony. Patricia said:

It was way up. They called it the buzzards' roost. My grandfather would say, "Watermelons will bloom in January before any of my children go to a movie theater where they have to go through the alley to get in the door." So we always saw movies long after they had been first run. But that was okay, they were new to us.

When Patricia was ten, her parents divorced. Erma Carwell took Patricia's younger brother, Nolan, who was born in 1951, and her younger sister, Sarah Frances, who was born in 1952, back to Nashville, Tennessee, where she got a job working at a hospital. Robert Carwell stayed in

St. Louis, as did Patricia, who went to live with her paternal grandparents.

Like Nashville, St. Louis was a segregated city. If Patricia and her family wanted to see a movie in St. Louis, they had to go all the way downtown to the Comet Theater, a cinema strictly for blacks.

Patricia said:

Patricia as a young girl.

As long as we were separated, there was this great mystique about white people. We labored under the misconception that all white people were smart, far better off than we were financially, and well-traveled. We were told through popular media that nobody of color was worthy of recognition. It was rare to see a black person on TV, in a commercial, or announcing the news. In magazines, our images were absent, except for *Ebony*.

13

I loved *Ebony* magazine because there were people
of color doing things on every page.

Many people in those days grew up with
incorrect ideas about other races. In a segregated
society, it was not a difficult conclusion to arrive
at. "It took a while to change those negative attitudes.
Stereotypes persisted," she said, "I got to see racism
up close and personal in my sixth grade year in
St Louis."

On May 17, 1954, the United States Supreme
Court outlawed racially segregated public schools
in the case *Brown* v. *Board of Education*. Patricia was
transferred to Robinson Elementary School, where
she was the only black child in her class.

"I learned that white people are not smarter
than we are. They're no cleaner than we are,
and they're no dirtier than we are either. They're
people," she said. "It was a very important year in
my life because a lot of the attitudes I have now
were shaped by that experience." She wrote about
those events in *A Friendship for Today*.

"I had the most wonderful teacher in sixth
grade," said Patricia.

Fredrick McKissack, second from left, with his third-grade class. Both the McKissacks attended segregated schools as young children.

Her name was Mrs. Elise Harvey, and wherever she is today, she deserves wings. She was white, yet she set the tone for that sixth grade year. She recognized that this was going to be a very difficult year for everybody—not just me, but for every student who was in that school, both black and white. The only problem for me was that I did not test well, so they put me in remedial classes where I could improve my skills. But I did not belong in those classes. I remember Mrs. Harvey saying I did not need special training. In her class, I was an honor student. I made good grades.

Patricia had beautiful penmanship, so Mrs. Harvey would have her write the date and the word of the day on the chalkboard. Patricia also had a good speaking voice, and she would often make class announcements. Mrs. Harvey acknowledged Patricia's skills and talents, and so the other children in her class were more accepting of her.

Patricia said:

I was an athlete and that put me in with the boys. I played softball and dodgeball. We also played racing games, and I loved volleyball. I also loved to dance. There were a couple of sweet girls, but it was friendship for the day, while I was at school. Just enough to get me through, without me being terribly lonely. After school, however, I would come back home to the black community and hang out with my friends in the neighborhood.

Someplace Special

$\mathcal{I}$n 1959, Patricia moved back to Nashville to live with her mother and her siblings. The McKissacks were a well-known family in Nashville, and Patricia became acquainted with the four McKissack brothers. One of them was Fredrick. "I knew about him," she said. "He was an older boy—five years older. I thought he was nice looking, but that was about it."

Every day after school, Patricia, Nolan, and Sarah Frances went to their maternal grandparents' house until their mother finished work.

We did not know that my grandfather, who we called Daddy James, could not read or write,

Patricia McKissack's grandparents, Frances Vinson, known for her cooking and her good homemade ice cream, and James Oldham, a storyteller, photographed around 1960.

because he always held the newspaper as if he was reading it. He was looking at the pictures, but we didn't know that. My grandmother was the one who could read. She had graduated from Pearl High School as well. I don't think my grandfather ever went to school, but he knew enough. He was a man of great dignity. He was tall and carried himself proud.

Daddy James was a master storyteller who told stories about two little girls and a little boy who were always having adventures. "We thought we were just as smart and clever and creative as those kids in Daddy James's stories," said Patricia.

His stories were all little lessons, but we never realized that until we were older. The stories had our names in them, and the children in the stories

Patricia McKissack's grandparents' house in Nashville, Tennessee, where she heard Daddy James's stories.

were always doing exciting things in the woods or by the river, like outsmarting crocodiles. We thought we could do that, too.

Patricia drew on Daddy James's stories when she wrote *Flossie and the Fox*. In her grandfather's tale, there were three little children who were confronted by a bear, a fox, a wolf, and a snake. "That's the way I originally wrote it," she said.

My editor, Anne Schwartz, wrote back and said there is a story in there somewhere, but there is way too much going on. I thought I had to be true to my grandfather's version, but my editor said I should be true to its essence. I didn't have to write it word for word. I could still be true to the intent without involving all those characters.

Patricia rewrote the story with just one main character instead of three.

Anne was able to get me to see that I wasn't taking away from my grandfather's tale. I was making it better by putting it in a different setting. I took out the brother and the sister, and I kept me, although there's a little bit of my brother and a little bit of my sister in Flossie, too. I got rid of the wolf, the bear, and the snake, and I kept the fox because I liked the fox's voice. That's how Flossie came to be. My grandfather taught me I don't have to beat up an opponent. Just be smarter.

Patricia said that Pete Bruce, in *Porch Lies*, was Daddy James's alter ego. The character shows another side of her grandfather's personality. She said:

My grandfather was very devout in his faith. I said to him one day, "Daddy James, I cannot imagine you drinking whiskey. That's not true, is it? Did you really drink that much whiskey?" He said, "Oh, baby, Daddy James drank barrels of it." He was a wild one in his young days. So when he told us about Pete Bruce, I always believed it was him. But he used Pete Bruce to show us the importance of good character.

Patricia's grandmother Frances was the ghost storyteller. It is from her that Patricia got the ability to tell the "jump tale," a short scary folk story that is designed to make the listener jump with fright at the end. *The Dark-Thirty: Southern Tales of the Supernatural* was inspired by her grandmother's stories. It was a Newbery Medal Honor Book, and it won the Coretta Scott King Award.

As a young girl, Patricia loved to read. She enjoyed comic books, and *Superman* was her favorite. She liked Westerns and biographies, too. She loved poetry, especially the work of Langston Hughes. "His poems were real and they were about real people,"

Patricia at age nine with her grandmother Sarah Jane James. Pat lived with her grandparents after her parents divorced.

Book FACT

Grandmothers

Patricia's grandmothers knew each other long before her parents married. Her father's mother, Sarah, and her mother's mother, Frances, met in Nashville where they worked at the White Way Laundry, which backed up to the McKissacks' home. After a while, Sarah and Frances got a job cleaning rooms at the Tulane Hotel. Then they went to work at the Vultee Aircraft plant during World War II. Patricia said:

My grandmother sent my father down to Mamma Frances's house to get something, and my dad met my mother. He was seventeen and she was eighteen. During the war, people graduated from high school and got married, and that's what they did.

she said. "He made it look so effortless."

Patricia went to the Nashville Public Library every week to check out books. It was the only place in downtown Nashville that was integrated. She could even go in through the front door. "I've written about that in my book *Goin' Someplace Special*," said Patricia. It is an important book to me," she said, "because the library was such a special place for me." Illustrator Jerry Pinkney was awarded the Coretta Scott King Award for his artwork. Years later, when Fredrick and Patricia attended the first National Book Festival at the White House, where they met

President George W. Bush and Mrs. Laura Bush, they saw a Christmas tree ornament on Mrs. Bush's Christmas tree that had an illustration from *Goin' Someplace Special*.

As early as third or fourth grade, Patricia knew she wanted to be a writer. All through school she wrote plays and poetry. "I would read a book and wonder what if it didn't end the way it did, or what if the character did something else," she said. "I would put those characters into my own stories or I would rewrite other people's stories and have them end the way I wanted them to end." Patricia also loved to write about exotic places. "I would get out my World Book encyclopedia, and I would look up different places. Even then, I knew I had to do research." Patricia even loved doing book reports. In fact, she would do them for other people, all the way up through high school.

Pat, age eight. She was a book lover from the early grades on.

Chapter 4

Building Bridges With Books

Fredrick McKissack was born on August 12, 1939. His parents were Bessye Fizer McKissack and Lewis Winter McKissack. The McKissacks were well-known builders and architects in Nashville. Fred's father, grandfather, and uncles were talented men with vision. His grandfather was the first licensed black architect in the state of Tennessee. He designed and built schools, office buildings, churches, and colleges. During World War II, the McKissacks were hired by the government to build the Tuskegee Air Base, where the famed Tuskegee Airmen, a group of African-American pilots, were trained.

Fred's parents, Lewis Winter McKissack and Bessye McKissack.

"The McKissacks also designed and built Pearl High School, where Fred and I graduated," said Patricia. "Our children have a proud heritage in their name. Yet the McKissacks were admired because they were not pretentious. They never wore their success as a mantle of privilege."

When Fred returned from the Marine Corps, he enrolled in Tennessee State University at the same time as Patricia. "We went to college together," she said, "but we didn't see too much of each other."

Patricia wanted to study journalism, but the university did not offer it as a major program. "When I was growing up, I wanted to write for a newspaper or a magazine. My girlfriend was a very good artist. Our plan was for her to design clothes and for me to write articles."

Patricia took all the journalism courses the university offered. She also studied music. Eventually she took courses in education and majored in English. She was an honor student in all of her courses, but in her senior year, she needed help studying for a math test. Patricia asked Fred for some help with the algebra problems. "I was an engineering major," said Fred, "and my best possible scores were in mathematics."

"I told him that it was for somebody else," she said, "but when we finished, he said 'I hope you do well on your test.' He knew all the time!"

Fredrick McKissack's grandfather Moses McKissack III, the first licensed black architect in Tennessee, with his wife, Miranda, and their six sons, taken about 1925. Fredrick's father, Lewis Winter McKissack, is at top left.

26

"I helped her with the problems," said Fred, "and she got through her course and graduated."

Fred and Patricia did not see each other again until they met at a party shortly after he graduated in 1964 with a degree in civil engineering. "I thanked him for helping me with the math," said Patricia, "and I confessed that it was me that needed the help."

"We sat and talked the whole night," said Fred.

"Fred called the next day and asked if we could go out," said Patricia, "and I agreed to go. We finished each other's sentences, and we giggled at the same things. He was such a gentleman and a kind person."

Fredrick McKissack's great-grandparents, Moses McKissack II, a builder, and Dolly Ann Maxwell McKissack, photographed in the 1880s.

Just as Patricia was getting ready to graduate, several airline companies came to the university to recruit African-American women for jobs as flight attendants, or stewardesses, as they were referred to in those days. Patricia thought it would be exciting to see the world.

Patricia and Fred attended the same high school. Fred graduated in 1957, Pat four years later.

I always wanted to visit other places, and that's what appealed to me about being an airline stewardess. As a child, my family was too poor to travel, so I often opened the encyclopedia to different countries and studied the photography and the wonderful faces of people who lived in far away places.

Patricia interviewed with United Airlines and made plans to sign up for training in Chicago at the end of the school year. The weekend of graduation, Fred came in from Columbia, Tennessee, where he was working for a chemical company called Union Carbide. He and Patricia went out on another date. "He asked me to marry him," said Pat, "and I accepted." They decided to get married within the next few months.

Upon graduating from Tennessee State with a Bachelor of Arts degree in English in the summer of 1964, Patricia took a job teaching Spanish and English in Lebanon, Tennessee. She and Fred were married on December 12. In January, Fred went to work for the U.S. Army Corps of Engineers in St. Louis, Missouri, and Pat joined him there when the school semester ended.

The McKissacks' first son, Fredrick Lemuel, Jr., was born in December 1965. Their twins, Robert Lewis and John Patrick, arrived on February 28, 1968. St. Louis became home. Today, they live in Chesterfield, Missouri, a nearby suburb.

In 1968, Patricia went to work as an English teacher at the same junior high school she had attended as a girl in Kirkwood, Missouri. About twenty-five percent of the students at Kirkwood Junior High were African Americans. She wanted to teach her eighth grade English students about Paul Laurence Dunbar, an African-American writer whose poetry she enjoyed in her childhood.

However, Patricia was not able to find a biography of the author, so she wrote one herself. "It was the first narrative I ever disciplined myself to write," she said.

While she was teaching, Patricia attended Webster University, where she completed a master's degree in Early Childhood Literature and Media Programming. As a part of that program, she did an internship at Concordia Publishing. When Concordia's editor, Carol Greene, announced that

The McKissacks' sons. Fredrick (left) is a writer; John (center), a mechanical engineer, and Robert (right), a teacher.

she was leaving, she suggested that Patricia apply for the position. Although Patricia had not planned to leave teaching, she applied for the job and became the editor of Concordia's religious books for children.

Pat had spent about year in her new role when she went to Atlanta to attend the American Library Association conference. When she returned, she told Fred about how few books there were for African-American children, and he shared her concern.

Patricia left Concordia in 1980 and took a job teaching freshman composition at Forest Park Community College. "It was the period just before I became a full-fledged writer," she said. Then, at the waterfall in 1981, Fred encouraged Patricia to follow her dream to write full time.

"The first books we wrote were for a religious children's book publisher in Chicago," said Fred. Patricia said:

I was already working in that market. People knew me. It was a way in. I did about eight or nine books with religious publishers. It got my name on a book and it got me out there as an author. We won an award for two of the books, and we were

Little Chair— Big World

"There are always tremendous changes when you go from one field to another," said Fred.

I went from being a civil engineer, building industrial plants, reservoirs, and a dam to being interested in children's books. The only way I was going to really learn anything about it was to go to the children's library. The first thing I noticed there was that all the chairs were very small, and I was taken aback sitting on one of them. I think it was right there that I realized that if I could sit in that chair, I could probably go on, but if I couldn't sit in that chair, then I'd have to go back. And somehow I was able to sit down in the chair with all the children around and read what they were reading. There I was, sitting in a little chair, reading about such a big world.

honored in our field because the stories were told with accuracy and they were fun for kids to read.

Around that time, Patricia wrote a manuscript about the Apaches, an American Indian tribe. She showed it to a friend. Her friend liked the book and suggested that she send it to Fran Dyra, an editor at Children's Press. Although Dyra did not publish that book, she asked Patricia if she would like to do a biography of Martin Luther King, Jr. The McKissacks worked on the book together, Children's Press published it, and it received high praise.

"The best review was given by Mrs. Coretta Scott King," said Fredrick.

> We sent her a copy and she sent us a note of appreciation. The Atlanta library invited us down to Atlanta. We went to the King Center, where they had a small gathering and we signed our book. It was the most wonderful experience, especially for a new writer.

The McKissacks followed *Martin Luther King, Jr.: A Man to Remember* with books about Frederick Douglass, Mary McLeod Bethune, and Paul Laurence Dunbar.

"People wondered how I was able to complete so many books so quickly, but I had already written some of them for my eighth-grade students," Patricia said.

"Then we did *The Civil Rights Movement in America from 1865 to the Present*," said Fred. "It became the publisher's largest selling single book."

"We did a series of fairy tales, myths, and legends, as well," said Patricia. "They were done in very simple language for beginning readers." Those books came out of Patricia's college studies and her childhood love of those kinds of stories.

> I had a teacher in fifth grade who read Greek, Roman, and Norse mythology to us. Later on, I discovered African mythology, Chinese mythology, Indian mythology, and so on. I come from a family of storytellers, and I enjoy any story that lends itself to telling.

The first five years of writing children's books were tough years for the McKissacks, but what kept them going was their strong sense of the importance of their work.

"As Fred always says," said Patricia, "the job that we have will last even longer than his papa's buildings, because we build bridges with books rather than building bridges with bricks."

How They Write

The McKissacks work as a team. Patricia does the writing, and Fred's forte is getting information and checking facts. He is also instrumental in getting their ideas out to young people so they can have a better understanding of who they are and what they are about.

The McKissacks see ideas everywhere. Sometimes an idea just pops into their heads and they know exactly what they are going to do with it. They call that an Athena idea. Athena is a goddess in Greek mythology who was born fully grown. "That's the way *Messy Bessey* was for us," said Patricia. "Our cleaning lady called us Messy Besseys, and we said,

35

'That sounds like a children's book.' We went back and forth, line for line, and within forty-five minutes we had written *Messy Bessey*."

Another kind of idea is the "mustard seed" idea. A mustard seed is tiny, but it grows into a huge plant. Fred said:

> It starts out very small. Maybe it is an idea about a character or an idea for a piece of dialogue. It could be an idea for a short story, a joke, or a theme. We build on that, and we build and build and it grows and grows. At some point, the story becomes a whole piece.

Sometimes the McKissacks get ideas from other people. For example, their publisher suggested they

Patricia and Fred in their home office.

go to Gee's Bend, Alabama, to interview a group of very poor women who made beautiful quilts. From that experience, they wrote *Stitchin' and Pullin': A Gee's Bend Quilt.*

The McKissacks said that the first tool of a writer is a library in some form. Nowadays, they begin their research with the Library of Congress, the largest library in the world. The Internet makes it possible for them to gather information from their home office. They also travel to different places to investigate a subject they are working on. For example, one day when they were watching the History Channel on television, Patricia heard about a black man who was a whaling captain. They decided to find out more about him. She said:

Patricia's interest in quilts led to a new book: *Stitchin' and Pullin': A Gee's Bend Quilt.*

> We visited the Nantucket Whaling Museum and discovered a Captain Boston who was master of a whaling ship. I said, "We've got ourselves a book."

We stayed a month visiting Martha's Vineyard and Cape Mystic and Bar Harbor. We even went out to Portland, Oregon; San Francisco; Monterey; and Barbados to get as much information as we could.

The book that resulted from their research, *Black Hands, White Sails*, was another Coretta Scott King Award Honor Book.

Sometimes Fred does the photo research for a book, the way he did for *A Long Hard Journey: The Story of the Pullman Porter*, another recipient of the Coretta Scott King Award, and *Red-Tail Angels: The Story of the Tuskegee Airmen of World War II*. Patricia said:

Fred will find a bone about something that we're working on, and he will build on that bone until he has constructed a complete skeleton. It is my job, then, to put the meat on the bones— description, action, and character. Fred wants to make sure we cover certain information and that the book has a specific slant. I am mostly concerned with story. We have learned to argue for what is the best approach to say what we want to say to young readers. It's our method of trying to reach kids in the best possible way.

If a book is fictional, their process is different. Patricia reads the story to Fred and asks him how it sounds and how it makes him feel. "I do not want to know if the words are in the right place. That's not what my fiction is about," she said. Fred understands that very well.

Of all their books, Patricia said that Fred is partial to *Nettie Jo's Friends* because he loves the spirit of the little girl who never gives up. He thinks *Christmas in the Big House, Christmas in the Quarters* is the best book Patricia has ever written. It was a winner of the Coretta Scott King Award.

Patricia said:

Mirandy and Brother Wind is a very special book to me. It received the Caldecott for Jerry Pinkney's artwork. However, I really don't have a favorite book because I don't have a favorite child. I feel very warm about all of my books. They are like my children. I attend to the one that needs me the most.

Writers Write!

$\mathcal{P}$atricia is very organized and a hard worker. She sets weekly, daily, and hourly goals for herself. "If I get finished with chapter three at noon, then I can play the rest of the day," she said. "If I don't get finished with chapter three until midnight, I will be down in my office until midnight."

She believes that the way to become a writer is to write. She said:

> Writers write. The way a person learns how to write is by writing. The way a person learns to write better is by writing more. Have a story to tell and write it. If you want to write nonfiction, then

40

Patricia and Fredrick McKissack at the 1993 American Library Association conference, where two of their books received major awards.

research what you are interested in and write down the facts in an engaging way. It all boils down to the idea that writers must write. Writers, write. Writers! Write! Writers write? Yes, Writers write.

Back in 1981, when the McKissacks decided they would write just one book for children, it was not so they could win awards. They wanted to contribute something and make a difference, but they never realized how far they would come.

Patricia said:

We had no idea it was going to be of this magnitude. When we are asked if we know what we have done, we say "No," because our heads have been down doing it. Then every once in a

Award-Winning Books

The McKissacks' books have won many awards. Here are just a few of them:

Precious and the Boo Hag
(Patricia C. McKissack and Onawumi Jean Moss)
- Charlotte Zolotow Award Honor Book

Days of Jubilee: The End of Slavery in the United States
(Patricia C. and Fredrick L. McKissack)
- Coretta Scott King Honor Award, 2004

Goin' Someplace Special
(Patricia C. McKissack; illustrated by Jerry Pinkney)
- Coretta Scott King Award for Illustration, 2002

Black Hands, White Sails: The Story of African-American Whalers
(Patricia C. and Fredrick L. McKissack)
- Coretta Scott King Honor Award, 2000

Let My People Go: Bible Stories Told by a Freeman of Color
(Patricia C. and Fredrick L. McKissack)
- NAACP Image Award, 1999

Christmas in the Big House, Christmas in the Quarters
(Patricia C. and Fredrick L. McKissack)
- Coretta Scott King Award, 1995

Sojourner Truth: Ain't I a Woman?
(Patricia C. and Fredrick L. McKissack)
- Boston Globe–Horn Book Award for Nonfiction, 1993
- NAACP Image Award

The Dark-Thirty: Southern Tales of the Supernatural
(Patricia C. McKissack)
- Newbery Honor Award, 1993
- Coretta Scott King Award, 1993

Mirandy and Brother Wind
(Patricia C. McKissack; illustrated by Jerry Pinkney)
- Caldecott Honor Award, 1989
- Coretta Scott King Award for Illustration, 1989

Other awards:
- The Regina Award, 1998
- The Jane Addams Children's Book Award for Peace
- The Children's Choice Award

while, we look up and say, "Did we do all of that?"
Then we get back to what we are doing. It is not
time to step back and celebrate. There's still so
much that needs to be done.

In order to reach more children with their
books, the McKissacks have visited places where
there was not one black person in the whole county
and very few in the state. Patricia said:

We told the librarians that they need these books
more than they need them in the inner cities.
There are places where kids have no idea about

The McKissacks enjoy visiting schools to share
their stories with children.

other people except for what they see on television. They need to know that African Americans are more than what they see in the media.

One of Fred's favorite anecdotes is a story about Albert Einstein, who was asked by a group of reporters what he thought was important to humanity and what was needed to move humanity forward. Einstein replied, "Tell stories to your kids, and have your kids read stories." Then they asked him, "What else do you think we should be doing?" He said, "Tell your kids more stories."

"What was Einstein trying to tell them?" said Fred. "He was telling them about the power of story. That is what Patricia and I have tried to do and we hope that what we have done is for the good."

Selected Books

by the McKissacks

Selected Books by Patricia C. and Fredrick L. McKissack

- *Black Hands, White Sails: The Story of African-American Whalers*
- *Christmas in the Big House, Christmas in the Quarters*
- *Days of Jubilee: The End of Slavery in the United States*
- *Hard Labor: The First African Americans, 1619*
- *Let My People Go: Bible Stories Told by a Freeman of Color*
- *A Long Hard Journey: The Story of the Pullman Porter*
- *Messy Bessey*
- *Rebels Against Slavery: American Slave Revolts*
- *Red-Tail Angels: The Story of the Tuskegee Airmen of World War II*
- *The Royal Kingdoms of Ghana, Mali, and Songhay: Life in Medieval Africa*
- *Sojourner Truth: Ain't I a Woman?*

Selected Books by Patricia C. McKissack

- *Abby Takes a Stand*
- *The All-I'll-Ever-Want Christmas Doll*
- *Amistad: The Story of a Slave Ship*
- *Away West*
- *Color Me Dark: The Diary of Nellie Lee Love, the Great Migration North*
- *The Dark-Thirty: Southern Tales of the Supernatural*
- *A Friendship for Today*
- *Goin' Someplace Special*
- *The Honest-to-Goodness Truth*
- *Jesse Jackson: A Biography*
- *Look to the Hills: The Diary of Lozette Moreau, a French Slave Girl*
- *Lu and the Swamp Ghost (with James Carville)*
- *Ma Dear's Aprons*
- *A Million Fish—More or Less*
- *Mirandy and Brother Wind*
- *Nettie Jo's Friends*

- *Nzingha: Warrior Queen of Matamba, Angola, Africa, 1595*
- *Our Martin Luther King Book*
- *A Picture of Freedom: The Diary of Clotee, a Slave Girl*
- *Porch Lies: Tales of Slicksters, Tricksters, and Other Wily Characters*
- *Precious and the Boo Hag (with Onawumi Jean Moss)*
- *Run Away Home*
- *Stitchin' and Pullin': A Gee's Bend Quilt*
- *A Song For Harlem*
- *Tippy Lemmy*
- *To Establish Justice (with Arlene Zaremba)*
- *Where Crocodiles Have Wings*

. . . .

In addition, Patricia C. McKissack has written books with her three sons, Fredrick McKissack, Jr.; Robert McKissack; and John McKissack.

assassinate—To murder a public figure, such as a political
  leader.

devout—Deeply religious.

dignity—Awareness of one's own worth; marked by calm,
  control, and pride.

essence—The core or basic quality of someone or
  something.

forte—Somebody's strength or talent.

integrated—Open to people of all races.

segregated—Separated by race.

Books

McElmeel, Sharron L. *100 Most Popular Children's Authors.* Westport, Conn.: Libraries Unlimited, 1999.

McKissack, Patricia. *Can You Imagine?* Katonah, N.Y.: Richard C. Owen Publishers, 1997.

Internet Addresses

Meet the Authors: Patricia and Fredrick McKissack

<http://www.eduplace.com/kids/hmr/mtai/mckissack.html>

Reading Rockets: The life and times of Patricia and Fredrick McKissack

<http://www.readingrockets.org/books/interviews/mckissack/bio>

Index